YOUR KNOWLEDGE HAS

Adrian O'Gara

**Investigation into the Cryptographic Properties of
Elliptic Curves Defined over a Prime Field**

GRIN Publishing

Bibliographic information published by the German National Library:

The German National Library lists this publication in the National Bibliography; detailed bibliographic data are available on the Internet at http://dnb.dnb.de .

Imprint:

Copyright © 2014 GRIN Verlag GmbH
Print and binding: Books on Demand GmbH, Norderstedt Germany
ISBN: 978-3-656-94562-8

This book at GRIN:

http://www.grin.com/en/e-book/295698/investigation-into-the-cryptographic-properties-of-elliptic-curves-defined

GRIN - Your knowledge has value

Since its foundation in 1998, GRIN has specialized in publishing academic texts by students, college teachers and other academics as e-book and printed book. The website www.grin.com is an ideal platform for presenting term papers, final papers, scientific essays, dissertations and specialist books.

Visit us on the internet:

http://www.grin.com/

http://www.facebook.com/grincom

http://www.twitter.com/grin_com

Investigation into the Cryptographic Properties of Elliptic Curves Defined over a Prime Field

Adrian O'Gara

16th June 2014

Abstract

Elliptic curves, as used in cryptography, are essentially points bounded by a finite prime field which display group properties that facilitate their usage in a cryptosystem. The Discrete Log Problem (DLP) - based on a large prime order subgroup of $(\mathbb{Z}_p)^*$ - constitutes the essence of Elliptic Curve Cryptography (ECC) and can be summed up as such; find an integer, k, such that $Q = kP$ where $k = \log_p(Q)$ and $P, Q \in (\mathbb{Z}_p)^*$. Compared to the Integer Factorisation Problem - upon which RSA is constructed - the DLP achieves a greater level of complexity in terms of resistance to attack. This project seeks to describe the mathematical properties that enable ECC to outperform RSA, culminating in the construction of a software system to demonstrate ECC's ability to securely encipher and decipher files and text, according to the National Security Agency's (NSA) Cryptographic Interoperability Strategy (CIS) or Suite B Cryptography.

"One of the most singular characteristics of the art of deciphering is the strong conviction possessed by every person, even moderately acquainted with it, that he is able to construct a cipher which nobody else can decipher."

- Charles Babbage

Contents

List of Figures

List of Tables

List of Algorithms

1 Project Plan and Scope

1.1 To investigate the mathematical properties of elliptic curves as they relate to cryptography

Elliptic curves, as they relate to cryptosystems, have very little to do with ellipses or curves, but rather the algebraic structure of the curves over finite fields, and can be considered more a group of points on the curve that, abstractly, hold a topological equivalency to a torus, and have coordinates (x,y) which satisfy the following equation in general -

$$y^2 + a_1 xy + a_3 y = x^3 + a_2 x^2 + a_4 x + a_6, ...a_i \in GF \tag{1.1}$$

or more specifically for a Prime field -

$$y^3 = x^2 + ax + b \cdots\cdots x, y, a, b \in GF(p) \tag{1.2}$$

and a Koblitz binary curve -

$$y^2 + xy = x^3 + ax + 1, \in GF(2^m) \tag{1.3}$$

where the discriminant satisfies the following -

$$\Delta = 4a^3 + 27b^2 \neq 0 \tag{1.4}$$

A thorough analysis of curve construction will be conducted in order to gain a complete understanding of the cryptographic use of elliptic curves.

1.2 To analyse ECC as an alternate to RSA

A comparative analysis of ECC and RSA will be undertaken in order to fully understand the implications of continued use of RSA or the future adoption of ECC. Both systems will be scrutinized under key strength, resistance to attack and NSA/NIST recommendations.

1.3 To identify and select an appropriate elliptic curve for use in a cryptosystem.

The National Institute of Standards and Technology (NIST) recommends the use of 15 elliptic curves, five reside in the Prime field and ten in the Binary field, of which five are Koblitz curves. The recommended Prime field curves will be examined and compared to the requirements of the NSA's Suite B security requirements, after which a curve will be selected and justified.

1.4 To design and develop a cryptographic software system as a vehicle for this investigation

A Java based system is to be created that will provide the user with the ability to construct an aysmmetric cipher key pair based on Elliptic Curves and use the keys to encrypt and decrypt any desired file or text.

1.5 Plan

1.5.1 Semester 7

Component	1	2	3	4	5	6	7	8	9	10	11	12	13
Project Proposal	1	1	1										
Scope & Plan			1	1									
Literature Survey		1	1	1	1	1	1	1	1	1			
ECC versus RSA		1	1	1	1								
Curve construction			1	1	1	1	1	1					
Prime Field versus Koblitz Curve			1	1	1	1	1	1	1				
Curve Selection								1	1	1			
Software Requirements							1	1	1	1	1		
Design								1	1	1	1	1	
Oral Presentation													1

Table 1: Project Plan

1.5.2 Semester 8

Component	1	2	3	4	5	6	7	8	9	10	11	12	13
Software Development	1	1	1	1	1	1	1	1	1				
Develop Plan	1												
Create GUI		1											
Key Pair Generation Method			1	1									
Encryption Method					1	1							
Decryption Method							1	1					
Key import/export									1				
Testing			1	1	1	1	1	1	1	1			
Draft Dissertation											1		
Final Dissertation												1	
Oral Presentation													1

Table 2: Semester 8 Plan

- **Week 1:** A development plan will be created to manage the temporal and work units of the project. Note that, aside from the testing phase, which iterates repeatedly, all other phases proceed concurrently.

- **Week 2:** A GUI (Graphical User Interface) will be designed and constructed according to the requirements in 3.2.1. Note that minor changes may occur owing to aesthetics.

- **Week 3 - 4:** The key pair generation method(s) will be implemented. Both native and imported libraries will be used to achieve an Elliptic Curve Diffie Helman system. Code will be tested.

- **Week 5 - 6:** The encryption method(s) will be created using the generated/imported EC public key. Code will be tested.

- **Week 7 - 8:** The decryption method will be created using the generated/imported EC private key. Code will be tested.

- **Week 9:** The methods allowing the import or export of a key pair. Code will be tested.

- **Week 10:** Full integration testing will be conducted on all aspects of the code. A security audit will be conducted to assure secure coding techniques were successfully employed.

- **Week 11:** Draft dissertation will be completed and reviewed.

- **Week 12:** Final dissertation will be completed.

- **Week 13:** Prepare and conduct oral presentation.

2 Literature Survey

2.1 Introduction

Elliptic curves have been studied for hundreds of years, however the use of elliptic curves in cryptography was independently proposed by Koblitz and Miller in the 1980's. The cryptographic use of the curves centres around the properties that emerge when the curves are defined over a finite field, and thus form a group. The following literature survey seeks to describe the cryptographic properties of elliptic curves and the possibility of a replacement for RSA.

2.2 Mathematical construction of elliptic curves for use in a Cryptosystem

Formally, an Elliptic curve may be defined as -

$$E\,(F) = \{\infty\} \cup \{(x,y)\} \in F.F \mid y^2 + ... = x^3 + ... \mid \tag{2.1}$$

That is, an elliptic curve E defined over a finite field F is the union of the point at infinity and the coordinates (x,y) which belong to the subset of F.F and both x and y satisfy the general Weirstrass equation -

$$y^2 + a_1 xy + a_3 y = x^3 + a_2 x^2 + a_4 x + a_6, a_i \in GF \tag{2.2}$$

The modular discriminant $\Delta = 4A^3 + 27B^2 \neq 0$ If and only if there are no double roots, then the curve E can be used to form a group.

As elliptic curves are underpinned by group theory, given that, according to the Lagrange and Mordell theorems, a finite field of prime order is an abelian group, they adhere to certain group axioms. Given two points P, Q, in a finite prime field $(GF(p))$, there exists a third point $P + Q = R\ (mod\ p)$ and the following relations hold true for all P, Q, R in $(GF(p))$

- $P + Q = Q + P$- Commutative Law

- $(P + Q) + R = P + (Q + R)$- Associative Law

- $P + O = O + P = P$ where O is the point at infinity. This is the identity element of the group

- There exists $(-P)$ such that $-P + P = P + (-P) = O$ - This is the inverse of the group

- $P + Q + R = O$

- $P + Q + Q = O$

- $P + Q + O = O$

Accordingly, the points on the curve may be manipulated with group operations, point addition/doubling and scalar multiplication, and it is these operations that lie at core of elliptic curve cryptography.

Point addition, $P + Q$, and point doubling, $P + P = 2P$, are implemented as follows -

Let $P = (x_1, y_1)$and $Q = (x_2, y_2)$
If $P \neq Q$; then $P + Q = -R = (x_3, y_3)$; then $R = (x_3, -y_3)$
Thus (x_3, y_3) is given as -

$$x_3 = \lambda^2 - x_1 - x_2 \tag{2.3}$$

$$y_3 = \lambda\,(x_1 - x_3) - y_1 \tag{2.4}$$

If $P = Q$; then $P = P$; then $P + P = 2P = (x_3, y_3)$
Thus (x_3, y_3) is given as -

$$x_3 = \lambda^2 - 2x_1 \tag{2.5}$$

$$y_3 = y_1 + \lambda(x_1 - x_3) \tag{2.6}$$

where λ, the slope of the line through P and Q, is given by

$$\lambda = \frac{y_2 - y_1}{x_2 - x_1} \text{ If } P \neq Q \tag{2.7}$$

$$\lambda = \frac{3x_1^2 + a}{2y_1} \text{ If } P = Q \tag{2.8}$$

Then consider the following trivial examples for point addition and point doubling on a curve[1] -

Take the curve$(E)y^2 = x^3 - ax + b$ where $a = -3$ and $b = 7$
pick the points $P = (-1.62,\ 2.77)$ and $Q = (2.77,\ 4.47)$

$$\therefore \quad \lambda = \frac{4.47 - 2.77}{2.77 - (-1.62)} = \frac{2.7}{4.39} = 0.615$$
$$\Rightarrow \quad x_3 = 0.615^2 - (-1.62) - 2.27 = -1.01$$
$$\Rightarrow \quad y_3 = 0.615(-1.62 - (-1.01)) - 2.27 = 3.0$$
$$\Rightarrow \quad -R = (-1.01, 3.0)$$
$$\therefore \quad R = (-1.01, -3.0) \text{ -R is reflected on the y-axis - inversion}$$

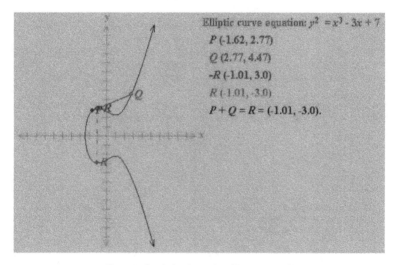

Figure 1: Graph showing point addition on an elliptic curve

---

[1]This example is trivial in that the arithmetic is not implemented in a finite field and would not be used in a cryptosystem. This is due to the infinite decimal expansion properties of $\mathbb{R}$ which would generate an inaccurate round-off error.

Point doubling is carried out in the following fashion -
Pick a point $P = (2.39, 3.67)$

$$\lambda = \frac{3(2.39)^2 + (-3)}{2(3.67)} = 1.92596$$
$$\Rightarrow \quad x_3 = 1.925926^2 - 2(2.39) = -1.09$$
$$\Rightarrow \quad y_3 = 1.925926(2.39 - (-1.09)) - 3.67 = -3.0$$
$$\Rightarrow \quad -R = (-1.09, -3.0)$$
$$\Rightarrow \quad R = (-1.09, 3)$$
$$\therefore \quad P + P = 2P = (-1.09, 3.0)$$

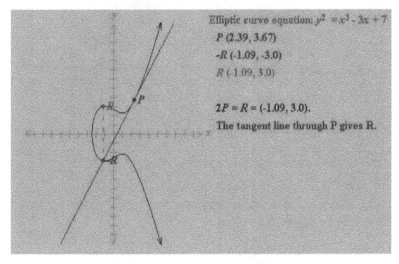

Elliptic curve equation: $y^2 = x^3 - 3x + 7$

P (2.39, 3.67)

-R (-1.09, -3.0)

R (-1.09, 3.0)

$2P = R = (-1.09, 3.0)$.

The tangent line through P gives R.

Figure 2: Graph showing point doubling on an elliptic curve

Scalar multiplication defines the process of obtaining a point kP by utilising a combination of both the point addition and point doubling operations in the fashion $P + P = 2P$, $P + 2P = 3P$ .....nP.

Consider the elliptic curve $E(GF_p)$ $y^2 = x^3 - (-3x) + 7 \ mod_7$
the following are the values for 7P -

$$(0, 0) \ (2, 3) \ (2, 4) \ (3, 2) \ (3, 5) \ (6, 3) \ (6, 4)$$

The previous example had a modulus of 7 and thus contains only a small number of points. Consider the following graph of the points on the curve $E(GF_p)$ with modulus of 929 , incidentally, a palindromic prime -

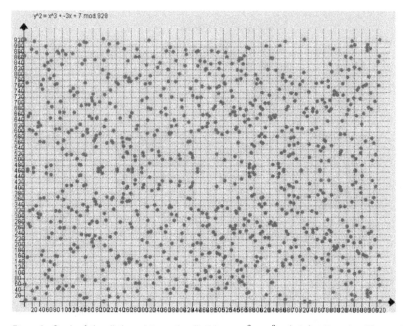

Figure 3: Graph of the all the points on the elliptic curve $y^2 = x^3 + (-3x) + 7 \ mod_{929}$ The graph was constructed in MATLAB

As can be seen in Figure 3, as the the modulus $p \to \infty$ the number of points increases dramatically and can be derived from Hasse's famous theorem -

Let E be an elliptic curve
$y^2 = x^3 - Ax + B$ with $A, B \in F(p)$
Then $|\#E(F_p) - (p-1)| \le 2\sqrt{p}$

When a sufficiently large value is selected for the modulus, the inverse operation, i.e. the discrete logarithm, becomes very hard to compute, with the best known algorithm, Pollard's modified $\rho - method$, [Gallant et al.(1999)Gallant, Lambert, and Vanstone] having a running time of $O(\frac{\sqrt{(\pi n)}}{2})$, where each iteration is one scalar multiplication.This intractability of scalar multiplication lies at the heart of the Elliptic Curve Discrete Logarithm Problem which in turn allows for the use of elliptic curves in cryptography. The ECDLP can be stated as such;

Let E be an elliptic curve over the finite field $GF(p)$ and let P and Q be points in $E(GF(p))$. The Elliptic Curve Discrete Logarithm Problem is in finding an integer, k, such that $Q = kP$ where $k = \log_p(Q)$.

Thus, elliptic curves may be modified for use in a discrete log cryptosystem. Diffie-Hellman is a key exchange protocol that utilises the discrete log problem as it's underlying hardness and is implemented with elliptic curves as follows;

Alice and Bob both agree on a random point, P, residing in a curve of $GF(p)$. Alice then chooses a secret value k_1 and computes the point $k_1 P$ and sends it to Bob. Bob, likewise chooses k_2 and computes $k_2 P$ sending it to Alice. The shared key then becomes $k_1 k_2 P$. An attacker would need to calculate the shared key knowing only P, $k_1 P$, $k_2 P$, this is the Diffie-Hellman discrete log problem for elliptic curves.[McGrew et al.(2011)McGrew, Igoe, Salter, Cisco Systems, and National Security Agency, ElGamal(1985)]

2.3 ECC as an alternate to RSA

Asymmetric key cryptography, such as ECC and RSA, utilise a mathematically linked public/private key pair for encryption and decryption. The public key, as the name suggests, is openly available to everyone and is used for encryption. The private key, known only to the user, is used for decryption. As shown previously, ECC relies on the discrete log problem in contrast to RSA, the most common asymmetric key algorithm, which uses the difficulty of factoring large primes as its underlying hardness, the so-called Factorisation Problem. Consider the following RSA key generation algorithm;

Algorithm 1 RSA key generation algorithm

Select two large primes p, q
Compute $n = pq$
Choose an integer e, such that $e > \varphi(n)$, $\gcd(e\varphi(n)) \equiv 1$,
where φ, Euler's Totient function $= (p-1)(q-1)$
e becomes the public exponent
Calculate $d = d^{-1} = e(mod\,\varphi(n))$ where d^{-1} is the multiplicative inverse
d is used as the private key

Supposing Bob wants to encrypt a message to Alice, he receives Alice's public key which consists of the prime modulus n and the public exponent e. Bob calculates $c = m^e(mod\,n)$, where c is the cipher text and m is the plain text, and sends c to Alice. In order to decrypt the message, Alice uses her private key d such that $m = c^d(mod\,n)$, thus obtaining the original message. If an attacker gains access to the modulus n and $\varphi(n)$ then factoring the modulus into p and q, which breaks the system, becomes trivial. Observe the following example, where the prime modulus n and $\varphi(n)$ are known;

$N = 768899$
$\varphi(n) = 767136$

let $p = \dfrac{n}{q}$, $q = \dfrac{n}{p}$, $n = pq$, $\varphi(n) = (p-1)(q-1)$

$\Rightarrow pq = 768899$, $(p-1)(q-1) = 767136$
$\Rightarrow pq - p - 1 + 1 = 767136$
$\Rightarrow 768899 - q + 1 - 767136 = p$

let $k = 768899 + 1 - 767136$
$\therefore k = 1764$

let $k - q = p$
$\Rightarrow 1764 - q = p$
$\Rightarrow 1764 - q = \dfrac{n}{q}$
$\therefore 1764 - q = \dfrac{768899}{q}$
$\Rightarrow 1764 - q^2 = 768899$
$\Rightarrow q^2 - 1764q + 768899 = 0$ $\therefore$ solve the quadratic -

$\Rightarrow \dfrac{1764 \pm \sqrt{(-1764)^2 - 4.1(768899)}}{2(1)}$
$\Rightarrow \dfrac{1764 + 190}{2} = 977$
$\Rightarrow \dfrac{1764 - 190}{2} = 787$

$\therefore p = 977$, $q = 787$
$\therefore q = 977$, $p = 787$

Integer factorisation, as shown, lies at the core of RSA and its difficulty can be described as such - Supposing an n-bit number that is the product of two large primes, there exists no known algorithm that can factor n in polynomial time $O(n \log n)$.

The best known method for factorisation is the General Number Field Sieve which has a running time of

$$((c + o(1))n^{\frac{1}{3}} \log^{\frac{2}{3}} n) \tag{2.9}$$

RSA-768, which has 232 digits, was successfully factored in 2009 by Thorsten Kleinjung et.al. However, the largest RSA prime, RSA-2048, has 617 digits and look set to remain secure until future advances in computational power or prime factorisation become available. Therefore, provided the key length is sufficiently large, RSA provides comparable security to ECC in terms of mathematical construction. It must be noted, however, that while ECC provides comparable security with RSA, the differences in key size are considerable. Consider the table below, it can be seen that for a 512 bit ECC key the comparable RSA key size is 15,360 bits. This fact is important when implementing a cryptosystem in a device with power or computational constraints, such as embedded systems, as competing resources may have an adverse affect on the operational status of the device thus breaking the security triangle of authentication, availability and integrity.

ECC Key size (bits)	RSA key size (bits)	Key size ratio	Symmetric key size (bits)
160	1024	1:6	80
224	2048	1:10	112
256	3072	1:15	128
384	7680	1:20	192
512	15360	1:30	256

Table 3: NIST public key size recommendation for RSA and ECC

Resistance to attack is another area that sees ECC out-perform RSA. As was previously shown, ECC is susceptible to Pollards $\rho - method$ while RSA is susceptible to the General Number Field Sieve. The complexity of an attack against ECC, however, grows exponentially, $O(2^n)$ with the key size, in comparison to an RSA attack which only grows sub-exponentially $O(2^{\log n^{\log \log n}})$. This has implications for the future use of RSA due to the ever increasing level of computational power being brought to bear on breaking the systems, as continuously increasing the key size will eventually become infeasible due to computational overheads. ECC with its exponential increase, seems much more likely to remain secure, and baring some future mathematical breakthrough in the discrete log problem, should continue to scale with increasing demands.

The previous comparisons are given greater weight due to RSA's exclusion from the NSA's Cryptographic Interoperability Strategy (CIS) or Suite B Cryptography. The CIS sets out recommended cryptographic protocols for use in Secret, Top Secret and Sensitive Compartmented Information (SCI) environments. For the protection of Top Secret information, the NSA recommends *"AES with 256-bit keys, Elliptic Curve Public Key Cryptography using the 384-bit prime modulus elliptic curve as specified in FIPS PUB 186-3 and SHA-384 are required to protect classified information at the TOP SECRET level"*.[National Security Agency(2009)]

2.4 Elliptic curve parameter selection

As stated previously, NIST[National Institute of Standards and Technology(2010)] and the NSA recommends the use of the P-384 curve parameters for use in sensitive environments. Comparing P-384 with the RSA alternative, one can clearly see the difference in key strength, a 7,680-bit RSA key would be required to provide similar security. This difference allows for less channel overhead when exchanging keys over a comm link, and while the computational cost-per-bit is greater, due to the mathematical complexity of ECC, the extra security more than compensates.

As the NSA recommends the use of the P-384 curve for Top Secret data, it can be assumed that the security of the curve is sound, however it cannot rule out the possibility that there exists some inbuilt method for compromising the system which is known only to the NSA. This has not affected the choice of curve for this investigation as defeating the NSA is not an objective.

Listed below are the chosen curve parameters selected for use in an ECC prime field cryptosystem - ;

The prime modulus $P384 = 2^{384} - 2^{128} - 2^{96} + 2^{32} - 1$
$P = 394020061963944792122790401001436138050797392704654$
$46667948293404245721771496870329047266088258938001$
861606973112319

The parameter $a = P384 - 3$
$a = 3940200619639447921227904010014361380507973927046544$
$66679482934042457217714968703290472660882589380$
1861606973112316

The parameter b
$b = 2758019355995970587784901184038904809305690585636$
$1568521428707301988689241309860865136260764883745$
107765439761230575

The base point $G = (X_G, Y_G)$
$X_g = 2624703509579968926862315674456698189185292349$
$110921338781561590092551885473805008902238805397571978$
6650872476732087

$Y_G = 8325710961489029985546751289520108179287853048861$
$31559470920590248050319988441922443864376039294733$
3078086511627871

Base point G in hexadecimal
$X_G = $ aa87ca22 be8b0537 8eb1c71e f320ad74 6e1d3b62 8ba79b98
59f741e0 82542a38 5502f25d bf55296c 3a545e38 72760aB7

$Y_G = $ 3617de4a 96262c6f 5d9e98bf 9292dc29 f8f41dbd 289a147c
e9da3113 b5f0b8c0 0a60b1ce 1d7e819d 7a431d7c 90ea0e5F

The order q, of the point G and the curve group E
$q = 3940200619639447921227904010014361380507973927046$
$54466679469052796276593991132635693989563081522949$
13554433653942643

3 Requirements

3.1 Primary Software Functions

The software artefact for this investigation shall be an encryption/decryption system that utilises elliptic curves to provide the security. The system shall enable a user to construct a public/private key pair and to then encrypt/decrypt a document using this key pair. The key pair will be constructed using the Diffie-Helman Elliptic Curve protocol with encryption being carried out using the Elliptic Curve Integrated Encryption Scheme (ECIES) using the parameters described in 2.4. The system should show the user the generated key pair and store them in a secure key ring, the key pair should also be exportable. As the system is designed to be run on a desktop or laptop and not a mobile device, resource constraints and operational overheads are not an issue.

3.2 Functional Requirements

The following are the functional requirements for the elliptic curve cryptosystem and are centred around three areas,

1. Public/Private key pair generation,

2. Encryption

3. Decryption.

3.2.1 Public/Private key pair generation

- **FR01:** The user will be given a dialogue box containing fields that must be filled in order to generate a key pair.

- **FR02:** User must be able to enter a name which will be used to identify the owner of the key pair.

- **FR03:** User must be able to enter an e-mail address which is also used for identification.

- **FR06:** The system must store the generated key pair in a secure keyring.

- **FR07:** The system must allow the user to view the generated key pair.

- **FR08:** The system must allow the user to import a public key.

- **FR09:** The system must allow the user to import a private key.

3.2.2 Encryption

- **FR11:** The system must allow the import of the file to be encrypted. The file will be selected from the users machine.

- **FR12:** The system must have a field to allow user fed text to be encrypted instead of an imported file.

- **FR13:** The system must allow the user to select a target for the message from the current list of public keys.

- **FR14:** The system must allow the user to select a key to sign the encrypted file.

- **FR16:** The system must encrypt and export the resultant file to a location chosen by the user.

3.2.3 Decryption

- **FR17:** The system must allow the user to import a file to be decrypted.

- **FR18:** The system must have a field to allow user fed text to be decrypted instead of an imported file.

- **FR20:** The system must export the resultant file

3.3 Non-Functional Requirements

The following are the non-functional requirements for the elliptic curve based cryptosystem.

- **NFR01:** The system shall be designed using secure coding techniques. This will ensure no vulnerabilities interfere with the correct functioning of the system whilst also maintaining system integrity

- **NFR02:** The system shall have a clear and concise user interface, with areas for inputting and viewing text along with buttons to allow the user to select between generating a key pair and encryption/decryption.

- **NFR03:** The system shall be built on open source resources and thus be open source itself.

- **NFR04:** The system should be user friendly and be easily operable. A novice user should be able to utilise all features with ease.

- **NFR05:** The system shall be coded using the Java programming language.

4 Design

This phase of the document will describe the crypto system in terms of the three main requirements outlined in section 4 - public/private keypair generation, encryption and decryption. Class diagrams will first be described followed by sequence diagrams.

4.1 Class Diagrams

The following class diagrams show the Encryption, Decryption, KeyGen and Process Text methods, along with an overall class structure diagram.

4.1.1 Encrypt Class Diagram

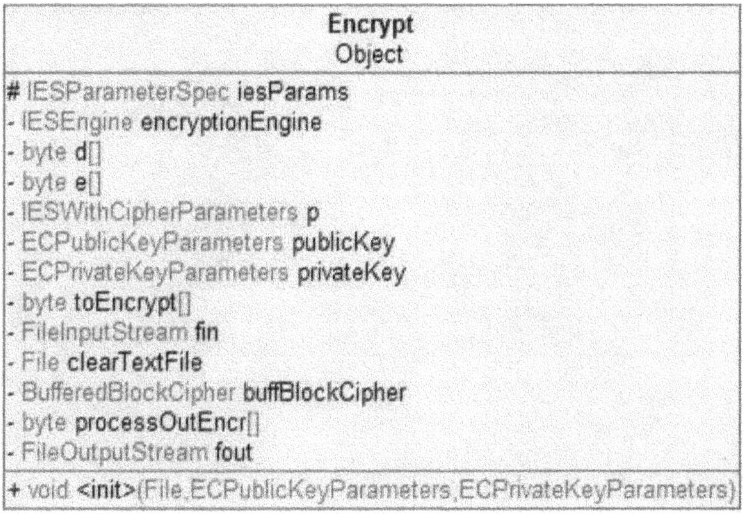

Encrypt Object
IESParameterSpec iesParams - IESEngine encryptionEngine - byte d[] - byte e[] - IESWithCipherParameters p - ECPublicKeyParameters publicKey - ECPrivateKeyParameters privateKey - byte toEncrypt[] - FileInputStream fin - File clearTextFile - BufferedBlockCipher buffBlockCipher - byte processOutEncr[] - FileOutputStream fout
+ void <init>(File,ECPublicKeyParameters,ECPrivateKeyParameters)

Figure 4: Encrypt Class Diagram

4.1.2 Decrypt Class Diagram

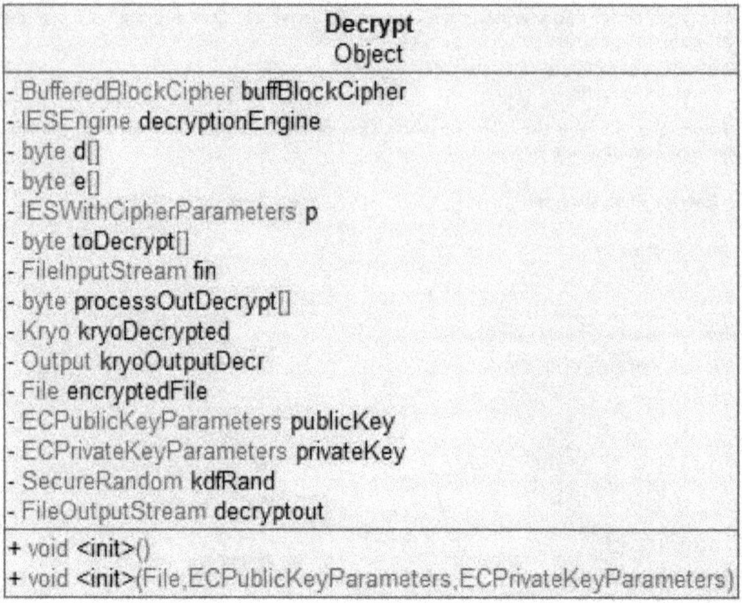

Decrypt
Object
- BufferedBlockCipher **buffBlockCipher**
- IESEngine **decryptionEngine**
- byte **d[]**
- byte **e[]**
- IESWithCipherParameters **p**
- byte **toDecrypt[]**
- FileInputStream **fin**
- byte **processOutDecrypt[]**
- Kryo **kryoDecrypted**
- Output **kryoOutputDecr**
- File **encryptedFile**
- ECPublicKeyParameters **publicKey**
- ECPrivateKeyParameters **privateKey**
- SecureRandom **kdfRand**
- FileOutputStream **decryptout**
+ void <init>()
+ void <init>(File,ECPublicKeyParameters,ECPrivateKeyParameters)

Figure 5: Decrypt Class Diagram

4.1.3 KeyGen Class Diagram

KeyGen
JFrame
- long serialVersionUID
- JPanel contentPane
+ JTextArea textArea
- JScrollPane scrollPane
- JLabel lblGenerateKey
- JButton btnExit
- JButton genKey
- ECDomainParameters domainParams
- ECKeyGenerationParameters keyGenParams
- ECKeyPairGenerator generator
byte userSeed[]
String name
KeyPairGenerator key
String email
String viewKey
- AsymmetricCipherKeyPair keyPair
+ ECPrivateKeyParameters privateKey
+ ECPublicKeyParameters publicKey
- byte privateKeyBytes[]
+ void main(String[])
+ String toHex(byte[])
+ String getPrivateKey()
+ String getPublicKey()
+ void \<init\>()
+ byte[] getUserSeed()
+ void setUserSeed(byte[])
+ byte[] getPrivateKeyBytes()
+ String getName()
+ void setName(String)
+ JRootPane access$0(KeyGen)

Figure 6: Key Generation Class

21

4.1.4 Process Text Class Diagram

ProcessText
JFrame
- long serialVersionUID
- JPanel contentPane
- JTextArea encryptTextArea
- File toEnc
byte encOut[]
- BufferedBlockCipher buffBlockCipher
- IESEngine encryptionEngine
- JTextArea decryptTextArea
- File decry
- String cipher
- String userCipher
- String plain
- KeyPairGenerator key
- ECPrivateKeyParameters privateKey
- ECPublicKeyParameters publicKey
- byte d[]
- byte e[]
- JButton btnDecryptText
- JButton btnEncryptText
- boolean isEncrypt
- byte encryptByte[]
- IESWithCipherParameters iesParams
- SHA512Digest shaDer
- SHA512Digest shaEncode
+ void main(String[])
+ void <init>()
+ void processText(boolean)
+ JTextArea access$0(ProcessText)
+ void access$1(ProcessText,String)
+ String access$2(ProcessText)
+ void access$3(ProcessText,byte[])
+ void access$4(ProcessText,String)
+ JTextArea access$5(ProcessText)
+ String access$6(ProcessText)

Figure 7: Encrypt/Decrypt Text

4.1.5 Class Structure

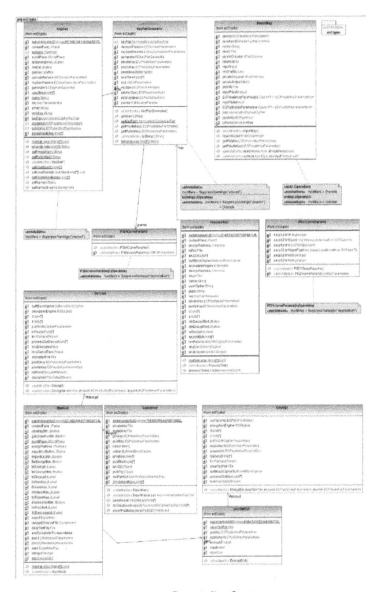

Figure 8: Class Structure

23

4.2 Sequence Diagrams

4.2.1 Process Text Sequence Diagram

Figure 9: Process Text Sequence Diagram

4.2.2 Encrypt Sequence Diagram

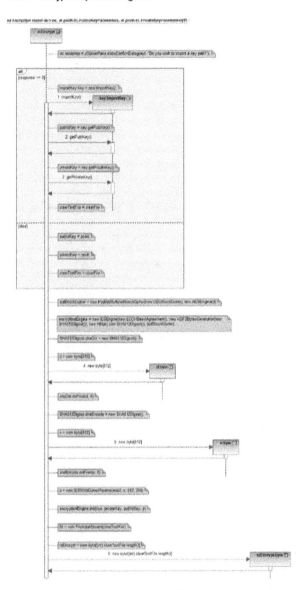

Figure 10: Encrypt Sequence Diagram

4.2.3 Decrypt Sequence Diagram

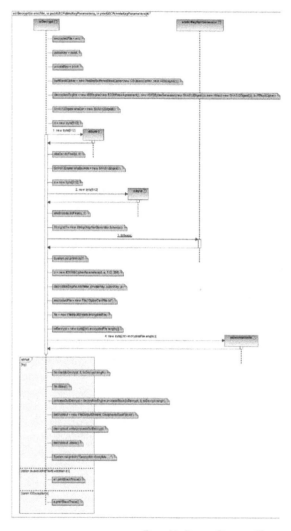

Figure 11: Decrypt Sequence Diagram

4.2.4 toHex method Sequence Diagram

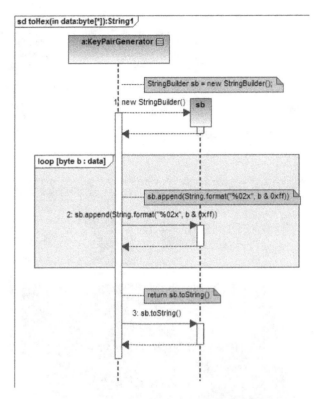

Figure 12: toHex Sequence Diagram

27

5 Implementation

5.1 Introduction

This section will detail the methods used to implement the cryptosystem as previously defined - see 3. Concerning the use of external libraries; It was noted that Java contains very limited native support for Elliptic Curve Cryptography, thus the decision was made to employ an external library - BouncyCastle - capable of providing the required features and free from licensing restrictions.

5.2 Week 1

An implementation plan was created. See 1.5.2

5.3 Week 2: Graphical User Interface (GUI)

As per section 3.3, the GUI was created to offer a clear and concise interface for the cryptosystem. Observe the main screen below:

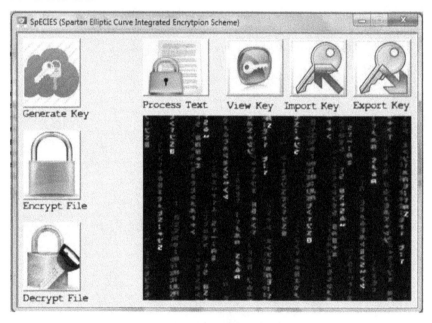

Figure 13: Main GUI window

As can be seen, there are 7 buttons, each of which corresponds to a unit of functionality as per section 3.2. The Generate Key button provides functionality for the generation of a private\public keypair and when pressed, opens an additional window to generate and display the keypair.

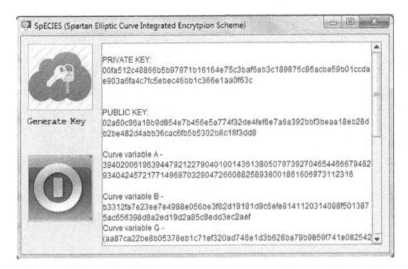

Figure 14: GUI showing the Key-Pair generator with generated keys.

The Process Text button allows the user to encrypt or decrypt text as per section 3.2.2 and is displayed below.

The encrypt button, provides a means to encrypt a file located in the users hard drive and contains a file chooser, encrypt button and exit button. See 3.2.2

Figure 15: GUI showing the Encrypt File function

29

The Decrypt File button allows for a previously encrypted file to be decrypted. The user selects the file from the hard drive. The View Key button allows the user to view the public and private keys along with the variables used to construct them. See 3.2.1

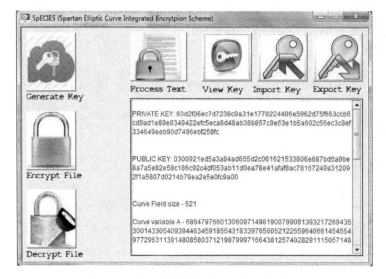

Figure 16: GUI showing the View Key function

5.4   Week 3 - 4: Key Pair Generation

In order to create the EC key pair the chosen curve - see 2.4 - must be defined in Java. A class was created called *'P384CurveParams'* which will be used to code the curve parameters. Observe the following:

```
@SuppressWarnings("deprecation")
protected X9ECParameters P384curveParams()
{
    // p = 2^384 - 2^128 - 2^96 + 2^32 - 1
    BigInteger secp384r1P = new BigInteger(
        "FFFFFFFFFFFFFFFFFFFFFFFFFFFFFFFFFFFFFFFFFFFFFFFFFFFFFFFFFFFFFFFFFFFFFFFF8000000000000000FFFFFFFF",
        16);
    // a, b
    ECCurve secp384r1Curve = new ECCurve.Fp(
        secp384r1P,
        new BigInteger(
            "FFFFFFFFFFFFFFFFFFFFFFFFFFFFFFFFFFFFFFFFFFFFFFFFFFFFFFFFFFFFFFFFFFFFFFFEFFFFFFFF0000000000000000FFFFFFFC",
            16),
        new BigInteger(
            "B3312FA7E23EE7E4988E056BE3F82D19181D9C6EFE8141120314088F5013875AC656398D8A2ED19D2A85C8EDD3EC2AEF",
            16));
    // x
    ECFieldElement secp384r1x = new ECFieldElement.Fp(
        secp384r1P,
        new BigInteger(
            "AA87CA22BE8B05378EB1C71EF320AD746E1D3B628BA79B9859F741E082542A385502F25DBF55296C3A545E3872760AB7",
            16));
    // y
    ECFieldElement secp384r1y = new ECFieldElement.Fp(
        secp384r1P,
        new BigInteger(
            "3617DE4A96262C6F5D9E98BF9292DC29F8F41DBD289A147CE9DA3113B5F0B8C00A60B1CE1D7E819D7A431D7C90EA0E5F",
            16));

    ECPoint secp384r1BasePoint = new ECPoint.Fp(secp384r1Curve, secp384r1x,
        secp384r1y, false);

    BigInteger secp384r1n = new BigInteger(
        "FFFFFFFFFFFFFFFFFFFFFFFFFFFFFFFFFFFFFFFFFFFFFFFFC7634D81F4372DDF581A0DB248B0A77AECEC196ACCC52973",
        16);
```

Figure 17: Code snippet showing the *P384 curve parameters*

The figure below shows the values returned by the *P384CurveParameters()* method:

```
byte[] secp384r1Seed = (Hex.decode("A335926AA319A27A1D00896A6773A4827ACDAC73"));
return new X9ECParameters(secp384r1Curve, secp384r1BasePoint, secp384r1n,
secp384r1h, secp384r1Seed);
```

Figure 18: Return values for the *P384CurveParameters()* method.

Above can be seen the parameters, p, a, b, x, y, n and $G(xG, yG)$, which were documented in 2.4, and are encoded using the *ECFieldElement* and *ECPoint* classes. The classes were imported from the BouncyCastle Library -

```
import org.bouncycastle.asn1.x9.X9ECParameters;
import org.bouncycastle.math.ec.ECPoint;
import org.bouncycastle.math.ec.ECCurve;
```

Figure 19: ECPoint and ECFieldElement classes

31

These parameters were then used to create an *X9ECParameters* object.[2] The variable *domainParams* - an *ECDomainParamaters* object - is used to create the parameters needed to construct the key pair.

```
P384CurveParams parms = new P384CurveParams();
X9ECParameters ecp = parms.P384curveParams();
domainParams = new ECDomainParameters(ecp.getCurve(),ecp.getG(),ecp.getN(),
ecp.getH(), ecp.getSeed());
```

Figure 20: ECDomainParameters construction.

The *ECKeyGenerationParameters* object , which will be used to initialise the *KeyPairGenerator*, is created in the following fashion -

```
keyGenParams = new ECKeyGenerationParameters(domainParams, new SecureRandom());
ECKeyPairGenerator generator = new ECKeyPairGenerator();
AsymmetricCipherKeyPair keyPair = generator.generateKeyPair();
```

Figure 21: Initialising the *KeyPairGenerator*

In order to extract the private and public keys from the key pair - remembering from 2.3 that they are mathematically linked - the following code was used:

```
privateKey = (ECPrivateKeyParameters) keyPair.getPrivate();
publicKey = (ECPublicKeyParameters) keyPair.getPublic();
privateKeyBytes = privateKey.getD().toByteArray();
```

Figure 22: Private and public key extraction.

The *privateKey* and *publicKey* variables are *ECPrivateKeyParameters* and *ECPublicKeyParameters* objects respectively. The need to cast the objects occurs as a result of the method *keyPair.getPrivate()* which returns an *AsymmetricKeyParameter* - a super-class of *ECKeyParameters*. The following is an example of an Elliptic Curve Private\Public Key Pair created using the P384 curve:

PRIVATE KEY:
009b297c01cea9e43358d39a297fee1b7d0795ad8c1409841ad
32220bc5e545398a24d5f52ed4292bc8bf08096538bbda2

PUBLIC KEY:
03c3e212dc8769a373cb8da0f4dc53029219bfc0e198bbb0e05
e821c889713f6832966fb88f0771c51f9eb72cfe127597c

Figure 23: Private and Public Key examples.

---

[2]See ANSI X9.62–2005 - Public Key Cryptography for the Financial Services Industry

5.5 Weeks 5 - 7: Encryption

As there is no direct method yet available for Elliptic Curve encryption, an alternate solution was applied. First a Buffered Block Cipher object was created, this was then used to wrap a Cipher Block Chaining object with an AES encryption engine. Cipher block chaining is a method of block encryption whereby each block depends on the Initialisation Vector (IV) - which provides semantic security and is essentially a zombie cipher block - and the preceding cipher block; each block in the chain is XOR'd with the preceding block and then encrypted. If a single bit in any block in altered the entire chain will become corrupted and undecipherable.

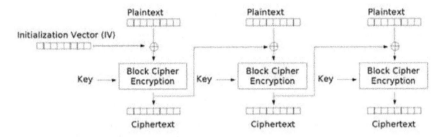

Cipher Block Chaining (CBC) mode encryption

Figure 24: Cipher Block Chaining

The CBC was implemented in Java as follows:

```
BufferedBlockCipher buffBlockCipher = new PaddedBufferedBlockCipher(new
CBCBlockCipher(new AESEngine()));
```

Figure 25: Cipher Block Chaining

The *buffBlockCipher* variable is now ready to be passed into the encryption engine, which will be an IESEngine and will be used to wrap the *buffBlockCipher* with 3 digest algorithms and a key agreement scheme - Elliptic Curve Diffie-Helman.

```
IESEngine encryptionEngine = new IESEngine(new ECDHBasicAgreement(),
new KDF2BytesGenerator(new SHA512Digest()), new HMac(new
SHA512Digest()), buffBlockCipher);
```

Figure 26: Encryption engine

As can be seen above, the *buffBlockCipher* object is wrapped in a SHA512 initiated Hmac - Hashed Message Authentication - which is then used to seed a *KDF2BytesGenerator* - Key derivation function. The encryption engine is now ready to be initiated. In order to do so, a set of cipher parameters needs to be defined. The following code creates the derivation and encoding function by using a SHA512 digest.

```
SHA512Digest shaDer = new SHA512Digest ();
byte [] d = new byte [512];
shaDer . doFinal (d, 0);

SHA512Digest shaEnc = new SHA512Digest ();
byte [] e = new byte [512];
shaDer . doFinal (e, 0);
```

Figure 27: Derivation and Encoding functions

The cipher parameters are initialised using the derivation and encoding functions along with the mac key size and cipher key size - which in this case in 256 as we are using AES256.2.3

```
IESWithCipherParameters p = new IESWithCipherParameters (d, e, 512, 256);
```

Figure 28: Cipher Parameters

The encryption engine can now be initialised using the cipher parameters and the private\public key pair: The boolean variable *true* is used to denote whether the method is for encryption or decryption.

```
IESEngine encryptionEngine . init (true, privateKey, publicKey, p);
```

Figure 29: Initialising the Encryption Engine

The actual encryption can now commence. Firstly, a byte array is created and the clear text file is encoded therein, then the encryption engine processes the file - the encryption. The resultant byte array is then written to the file system with the suffix '.enc'.

```
FileInputStream fin = new FileInputStream (clearTextFile);
byte [] toEncrypt = new byte [(int) clearTextFile . length ()];
fin . read (toEncrypt);
fin . close ();

byte [] processOutEncr = encryptionEngine . processBlock (toEncrypt, 0, toEncrypt . length);

fout = new FileOutputStream (clearTextFile . getAbsolutePath () + ".enc");
fout . write (processOutEncr);
fout . flush ();
fout . close ();
```

Figure 30: The file byte array is encrypted and saved to the file system.

5.6   Week 8: Decryption

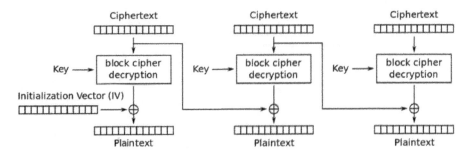

Cipher Block Chaining (CBC) mode decryption

Figure 31: CBC Decryption

The decryption method is almost identical to the encryption method, save for the boolean variable - which denotes encryption or decryption - in 29.

IESEngine decryptionEngine.init(false, privateKey, publicKey, p);

Figure 32: Decryption initialiser.

byte [] processOutDecrypt = decryptionEngine.processBlock(toDecrypt, 0,toDecrypt.length

Figure 33: Decrypted byte array.

5.7   Week 9: Key Import/Export

As the method for constructing the key pair relied upon external libraries, the project was beholden to the restrictions placed by the library authors. These included the non-serialisable nature of the classes that produced the key pair and the lack of default constructors, additionally the libraries contain no support for a key store in which to contain the keys, were one able to export them.
. An attempt was made to bypass the restrictions by employing an external library called Kryo. This library wraps objects in a Kryo object and attempts to export the resultant new object. This method was successful in exporting the keys and was implemented as follows -

```
public byte[] serialize(Object object)
{
        try
        {
                ByteArrayOutputStream stream = new ByteArrayOutputStream();
                // FileOutputStream stream = new FileOutputStream("test");
                Output output = new Output(stream);
                // stream.flush();
                // stream.close()
                output.close();
                return stream.toByteArray();
        }
        catch (IOEXception ioex)
        {
                ioex.printStackTrace();
        }
```

Figure 34: Key import/export attempt

The problem arose, however, during the import stage. As the keys were exported to a byte array, and a File object, they were imported as one too. Kryo looked for a default constructor with which to create the imported object and, of coarse, there was none, due to the nature of the key pair - see 5.4

```
inKey = publicChooser.getSelectedFile();
input = new Input(new FileInputStream(inKey));

publKey=(crypto.params.ECPublicKeyParameters)kryoPublic.readClassAndObject(input);
```

Figure 35: Kryo import method.

6 Conclusion

6.1 Evaluation

Currently Elliptic Curve Cryptography is in it's infancy, commercially at any rate, and as such has not had the wide spread developer attention that RSA enjoys. Internal Java support for ECC is limited at best, so the decision was made to utilise an external library to provide the necessary support for the project. BouncyCastle was chosen for two reasons; it was an open source library and it contained all the necessary tools to construct the cryptosystem. However, it would be preferable for one to construct the libraries from scratch, the reasoning being that imported libraries are inherently insecure as they were written by, essentially, persons unknown, and could contain any number of features designed to subvert the security of the system - as was stated in ?? - or allow the writer dangerous knowledge of all cryptosystems developed using the libraries. Developing the libraries from the ground up would also alleviate the problem of key import and export and would allow the creation of a dedicated key store in which to securely store them. At present both these features are lacking in the appropriate available libraries.

Ultimately the project was a success; Elliptic curves were utilised to create a cryptosystem capable of securely enciphering and deciphering files and text. Best practices were followed according to the NSA's Cryptographic Interoperability Strategy (CIS) or Suite B Cryptography.[National Security Agency(2009)] While a far cry away from a commercial application, the developed system shows that a viable replacement - Elliptic Curve Cryptography (ECC) - for RSA is achievable and demonstrably superior in the role - see 2.3

6.2 Further Work

Cryptography's raison d'être, as was shown, is to encipher and decipher information and is traditionally deployed as a defensive measure, a method to protect and conceal. Consider then an alternate deployment, where-by cryptography is used as an offensive weapon, a method to effectively hold data for ransom, as was seen with the Cryptolocker virus, or as an area-denial weapon - a cyber equivalent to an artillery barrage. Weaponised cryptography has the potential to cause devastating damage to global internet infrastructure. An attacker could offensively deploy a cryptographic payload to multiple critical internet nodes, encrypting the entire contents of swaths of the internet which would result not only in loss of data, but would also see global internet traffic grind to a halt. Thus it is clear that while highly secure cryptographic protocols are increasingly more desirable, care must be taken to examine the implications of creating such protocols and conduct research into defensive measures lest they be turned against us; As Dr. Frankenstein lamented *"When I reflected on his crimes and malice, my hatred and revenge burst all bounds of moderation. I would have made a pilgrimage to the highest peak of the Andes, could I when there have precipitated him to their base."*[Shelly(2007)]

References

[ANSI(1998)] ANSI, Jul. 1998. Public key cryptography for the financial services industry: Elliptic curve key agreement and key transport schemes. Tech. Rep. Version 2.

[Centicom Research(1999)] Centicom Research, Oct. 1999. Recommended elliptic curve domain parameters.

[ElGamal(1985)] ElGamal, T., 1985. A public key cryptosystem and a signature scheme based on discrete logarithms. IEEE Transactions on Information Theory 31, 469–472.

[Gallant et al.(1999)Gallant, Lambert, and Vanstone] Gallant, R., Lambert, R., Vanstone, S., May 1999. Improving the parallelized pollard lambda search on anamalous binary curves. Mathematics of Computation 69 (232), 1699–1705.

[Guajardo and Paar(1997)] Guajardo, J., Paar, C., 1997. Efficient algorithms for elliptic curve cryptosystems. Lecture Notes in Computer Science 1294, 342–356.

[Hankerson et al.(2000)Hankerson, Hernandez, and Menezes] Hankerson, D., Hernandez, J. L., Menezes, A., 2000. Software implementation of elliptic curve cryptography over binary fields. Cryptographic Hardware and Embedded Systems, 1–24.

[ISO/IEC 15946(1999)] ISO/IEC 15946, 1999. Information technology - security techniques - cryptographic techniques based on elliptic curves. Committee draft.

[Joye and Tymen(2001)] Joye, M., Tymen, C., 2001. Protections against differential analysis for elliptic curve cryptography - an algebraic approach. Cryptographic Hardware and Embedded Systems 2162 (Lecture Notes in Computer Science), 377–390.

[Kapoor et al.(2008)Kapoor, Abraham, and Singh] Kapoor, V., Abraham, V. S., Singh, R., May 2008. Elliptic curve cryptography. ACM Ubiquity 9 (20).

[Koblitz(1987)] Koblitz, N., Jan. 1987. Elliptic curve cryptosytems. Mathematics of Computation 48 (177), 203–209.

[Koblitz(1989)] Koblitz, N., 1989. Hyperelliptic cryptosystems. Journal of Cryptology 1, 139–150.

[Koblitz(1993)] Koblitz, N., 1993. Introduction to Elliptic Curves and Modular Forms, 2nd Edition. Springer-Verlag.

[Koblitz et al.(2000)Koblitz, Menezes, and Vanstone] Koblitz, N., Menezes, A., Vanstone, S., 2000. The state of elliptic curve cryptography. Designs, Codes and Cryptography 19, 173–193.

[McGrew et al.(2011)McGrew, Igoe, Salter, Cisco Systems, and National Security Agency] McGrew, D., Igoe, K., Salter, M., Cisco Systems, National Security Agency, Feb. 2011. Fundamental elliptic curve cryptography algorithms. Tech. Rep. RFC 6090, IETF.
URL http://tools.ietf.org/html/rfc6090

[National Institute of Standards and Technology(2007)] National Institute of Standards and Technology, Mar. 2007. Recommendation for pair-wise key establishment schemes using discrete logarithm cryptography (revised). Special publication 800-56A.

[National Institute of Standards and Technology(2010)] National Institute of Standards and Technology, Apr. 2010. Mathematical routines fo the NIST prime elliptic curves. Tech. rep., NIST.
URL http://www.nsa.gov/ia/_files/nist-routines.pdf

[National Security Agency(2009)] National Security Agency, 2009. Suite b cryptography.
URL http://www.nsa.gov/ia/programs/suiteb_cryptography/

[Shelly(2007)] Shelly, M., 2007. Frankenstein, illustrated, annotated Edition. Infobase Publishing.

[Thijssen(2010)] Thijssen, J., Dec. 2010. Encryption operating modes: ECB vs CBC.
URL https://www.adayinthelifeof.nl/2010/12/08/encryption-operating-modes-ecb-vs-cbc/